J. E. C Chapman

Easter hymns

J. E. C Chapman

Easter hymns

ISBN/EAN: 9783741183027

Manufactured in Europe, USA, Canada, Australia, Japa

Cover: Foto ©Angelika Wolter / pixelio.de

Manufactured and distributed by brebook publishing software (www.brebook.com)

J. E. C Chapman

Easter hymns

1876.

Introduction.

AMONG the encouraging hopes in these days of doubt and unbelief, the increasing observance of the great festivals of the Church by all within the circle of her influence is certainly one of the strongest. Each year, as the seasons come round, they make a stronger appeal, and meet a heartier response. Most especially is this true of Easter, that "day of days." Its sun shines with fuller radiance each year upon the world, whose night of darkness it broke on the Resurrection Morning. The anthems which greet its rising are caught and repeated by increasing millions of grateful hearts of every tongue, kindred, and people, until the wide earth is filled with their sounding praise. How sacred a privilege to have part in this mighty and triumphant symphony, how sad to be out of harmony with its sublime strains!

As a humble offering of grateful love to the risen Lord, this collection of hymns, full of the spirit of the Easter joy, is sent forth. It makes no pretension to any thoroughness of research; but as one going through the field plucks here and there, until a small but rich sheaf fills his hand, so have these hymns been gathered and bound together. That the precious seed they carry may spring up and bear immortal fruit where they may chance to fall, is the reward she asks by whose hand they have been collected.

J. I. T. COOLIDGE.

ST. MARK'S, SOUTHBOROUGH,
    March, 1876.

Table of First Lines.

	PAGE.
Again the Lord of life and light	86
Alleluia! Alleluia!	127
Angel, roll the stone away	99
A pathway opens from the tomb	82
As spring's sweet breath after long wintry snow	84
At the Lamb's high feast we sing	28
Awake, thou wintry earth	21
Blest morning whose young dawning rays	63
Christ has arisen	137
Christ hath arisen	113
Christ is risen, Christ is risen.	133
Christ the Lord is risen again	31
Christ the Lord is risen to-day	61
Christ the Lord is risen to-day	68
Come, see the place where Jesus lay	102
Come, ye faithful, raise the strain	35
Come, ye saints, look here and wonder	87

	PAGE.
Days grow longer, sunbeams stronger	131
Death and darkness, get you packing	12
Do saints keep holy-day in heavenly places?	88
Hail, day of days! in peals of praise	57
Hallelujah! Hallelujah!	33
Hark! the angels bright are singing	135
He is risen, He is risen	104
How shall we keep this holy day of gladness?	107
In the bonds of death He lay	50
I say to all men far and near	91
Jesus Christ is risen to-day	30
Jesus lives: no longer now	78
Let the merry church-bells ring	121
Lift your glad voices in triumph on high	101
Light's glittering morn bedecks the sky	47
Lord, who createdst man in wealth and store	43
Mary to her Saviour's tomb	93
Morning breaks upon the tomb	90
Most glorious Lord of lyfe that on this day	11
O glorious Head, Thou livest now	55
Oh, day of days! shall hearts set free	95
O risen Lord, O conquering King	65
O sons and daughters, let us sing	45
Our Lord is risen to-day	109

	PAGE.
Purge we out the ancient leaven.	37
Rise, heart, thy Lord is risen: sing His praise	41
Rise, heire of fresh eternity	25
Sleep, sleep, old sun: thou canst not have re-past	15
Still thy sorrow, Magdalena	59
Sun, shine forth in all thy splendor	73
Sweetly are the birds singing.	123
The day of resurrection	53
"The Lord is risen indeed".	77
The Lord of life is risen	118
The setting orb of night her level ray	19
The strife is o'er, the battle done	105
The world itself keeps Easter Day	125
This is the feast-day of our King	129
Thou whose sad heart and weeping head lyes low	27
Unchanged through all the changing years.	116
Up and away.	17
Welcome, thou Victor in the strife	71
What glorious light	23
Who from the fiery furnace saved the three	13
Yes, the Redeemer rose	80

"Now is Christ risen from the dead
and become the
firstfruits of them that slept."

> "Thou hast ascended on high, thou hast led
> captivity captive."

Most glorious Lord of lyfe that on this Day,
Didst make Thy Triumph over Death and Sin;
And, having harrow'd Hell, didst bring away
Captivity thence Captive, us to win:
This joyous Day, deare Lord, with Joy begin;
And grant that wee for whom thou diddest dy,
Being with Thy deare Blood clene washt from Sin,
May live for ever in felicity!
And that Thy love we weighing worthily,
May likewise love Thee for the same again,
And for Thy sake, that all lyke deare didst buy,
With Love may one another entertayne!
So let us love, deare Love, lyke as we ought:
Love is the Lesson which the Lord us taught.

EDMUND SPENSER.

"Salvation to our God, which sitteth upon the throne, and unto the Lamb."

DEATH and darkness, get you packing!
Nothing now to man is lacking;
All your triumphs now are ended,
And what Adam marr'd is mended;
Graves are beds now for the weary;
Death a nap, to wake more merry;
Youth now, full of pious duty,
Seeks in thee for perfect beauty;
The weak and aged, tir'd with length
Of daies, from thee look for new strength;
And infants with thy pangs contest
As pleasant as if with the brest.
   Then unto Him who thus hath thrown,
Even to contempt, thy kingdome down,
And by His blood did us advance
Unto His own inheritance,
To Him be glory, power, praise,
From this unto the last of daies.

HENRY VAUGHN.

"Now is Christ risen from the dead, and become the
first-fruits of them that slept."

Who from the fiery furnace saved the Three
   Suffers as a mortal ; that, His passion o'er,
This mortal, triumphing o'er death, might be
   Vested with immortality once more ;
      He whom our fathers still confest
      God over all, forever blest.

The women with their ointment seek the tomb ;
   And Whom they mourned as dead, with many a tear,
They worship now, joy dawning on their gloom,
   As living God, as mystic Passover ;
      Then to the Lord's Disciples gave
      The tidings of the vanquished grave.

We keep the festal of the death of death:
  Of hell o'erthrown: the first fruits pure and bright
Of life eternal; and with joyous breath
    Praise Him that won the victory by His might;
      Him whom our fathers still confest
      God over all, forever blest.

All hallowed festival, in splendor born!
  Night of salvation and of glory! Night
Fore-heralding the Resurrection morn!
    When from the tomb the everlasting Light,
      A glorious frame once more His own,
      Upon the world in splendor shone.

St. John of Damascus.
Translated by J. M. Neale.

"He rose again the third day."

Sleep, sleep, old sun! thou cans't not have re-past
As yet the wound thou took'st on Friday last.
Sleep, then, and rest: the world may bear thy stay.
A better sun rose before thee to-day;
Who, not content to enlighten all that dwell
On the earth's face as thou, enlightened hell,
And made the dark fires languish in that vale,
As at thy presence here our fires grow pale;
Whose body, having walked on earth and now
Hastening to heaven, would, that He might allow
Himself unto all stations and fill all,
For these three days become a mineral.
He was all gold when He lay down, but rose
All tincture; and doth not alone dispose
Leaden and iron wills to good, but is
Of power to make even sinful flesh like His.
Had one of those, whose credulous piety
Thought that a soul might discern and see

Go from a body, at this sepulchre been,
And issuing from the sheet this body seen,
He would have justly thought this body a soul,
If not of any man, yet of the whole.

Dr. Donne.

"If ye, then, be risen with Christ, seek those
things which are above."

Up, and away,
        Thy Saviour's gone before.
Why dost thou stay,
        Dull soule?   Behold the doore
Is open, and His precept bids thee rise,
Whose power hath vanquish't all thine enemies.
Say not, I live,
        Whilst in the grave thou ly'st!
He that doth give
        Thee life, would have thee prize't
More highly than to keep it bury'd where
Thou canst not make the fruit of it appeare.
Is rottennesse
        And dust so pleasant to thee,
That happinesse
        And heaven cannot wooe thee
To shake thy shackles off, and leave behind thee
Those fetters, which to death and hell did bind thee?

In vain thou say'st
>Th'art bury'd with thy Saviour,
If thou delay'st
>To shew, by thy behaviour,
That thou art risen with Him. Till thou shine
Like Him, how canst thou say His light is thine?
Early he rose,
>And with Him brought the day,
Which all thy foes
>Frighted out of the way.
And wilt thou sluggard-like turn in thy bed,
Till noon-sun beams draw up thy drowsie head?
Open thine eyes,
>Sin-seiled soule, and see
What cobweb tyes
>They are that trammell thee.
Not profits, pleasures, honours, as thou thinkest;
But losse, pain, shame, at which thou vainly winkest.
All that is good
>Thy Saviour dearly bought
With His heart's blood;
>And it must there be sought,
Where He keeps residence that rose this day.
Linger no longer then : up and away.

CHRISTOPHER HARVEY.

"I am the resurrection and the life."

The setting orb of night her level ray
Shed o'er the land ; and on the dewy sward
The lengthened shadows of the triple cross
Were laid far stretched, — when in the east arose,
Last of the stars, day's harbinger : no sound
Was heard, save of the watching soldier's foot.
Within the rock-barred sepulchre, the gloom
Of deepest midnight brooded o'er the dead,
The Holy One : but lo ! a radiance faint
Began to dawn around His sacred brow ;
The linen vesture seemed a snowy wreath,
Drifted by storms into a mountain cave ;
Bright and more bright the circling halo beamed
Upon that face, clothed in a smile benign,
Though yet exanimate. Nor long the reign
Of death ; the eyes that wept for human griefs
Unclose, and look around with conscious joy,
Yes ; with returning life, the first emotion

That glowed in Jesus' breast of love, was joy
At man's redemption, now complete ; at death
Disarmed ; the grave transformed into the couch
Of faith ; the resurrection and the life.
Majestical He rose : trembled the earth ;
The ponderous gate of stone was rolled away ;
The keepers fell ; the angel, awe-struck, sunk
Into invisibility, while forth
The Saviour of the world walked, and stood
Before the sepulchre, and viewed the clouds
Impurpled glorious by the rising sun.

JAMES GRAHAME.

"The Lord is risen indeed."

AWAKE, thou wintry earth,
   Fling off thy sadness ;
Fair vernal flowers, laugh forth
   Your ancient gladness :
      Christ is risen.

Wave, woods, your blossoms all,
   Grim Death is dead ;
Ye weeping funeral trees,
   Lift up your head :
      Christ is risen.

Come, see, the graves are green ;
   It is light ; let's go
Where our loved ones rest
   In hope below :
      Christ is risen.

All is fresh and new,
    Full of spring and light;
Wintry heart, why wear'st the hue
    Of sleep and night?
        Christ is risen.

Leave thy cares beneath,
    Leave thy worldly love;
Begin the better life
    With God above:
        Christ is risen.

THOMAS BLACKBURN.

"I know that ye seek Jesus which was crucified. He is not here; for He is risen."

    WHAT glorious light!
How bright a Sun after so sad a night
Does now begin to dawn! Bless'd were those eyes
    That did behold
This Sun, when He did first unfold
His glorious beams, and now begin to rise.
It was the holy, tender sex
    That saw the first ray:
Saint Peter and the other had the reflex,
    The second glimpse o' th' day.
Innocence had the first; and he
That fled, and then did penance, next did see
The glorious Sun of Righteousness
    In His new dress
Of triumph, immortality, and bliss.

O dearest God, preserve our souls
        In holy innocence!
Or, if we do amiss,
Make us to rise again to th' life of Grace,
That we may live with Thee and see Thy glorious face,
The Crown of holy penitence.
        Allelujah!

JEREMY TAYLOR.

"Thou wilt not leave my soul in hell, neither wilt thou suffer thine Holy One to see corruption."

Rise heire of fresh eternity
    From Thy virgin Tombe ;
Rise mighty man of wonders, and Thy world with Thee,
Thy Tombe the universall East,
    Nature's new wombe,
Thy tombe faire immortalities perfumed nest.

Of all the glories make noone gay,
    This is the Morne ;
This Rock buds forth the fountaine of the streames of
    Day ;
In joyes white annalls lives this houre
    When life was borne,
No cloud scoule on His radiant lids, no tempest lower.

Life, by this light's Nativity
      All creatures have,
Death onely by this Dayes just doome is forc't to Dye.
Nor is Death forc't ; for may he ly
      Thron'd in Thy Grave,
Death will on that condition be content to dye.
RICHARD CRASHAW.

"Who shall deliver me from the body of this death?
I thank God through Jesus Christ our Lord."

Thou, whose sad heart and weeping head lyes low,
   Whose cloudy brest cold damps invade,
Who never feel'st the sun nor smooth's thy brow,
   But sitt'st oppressed in the shade,
            Awake! Awake!
And in His resurrection partake,
   Who on this day, that thou might'st rise as He,
   Rose up, and cancell'd two deaths due to thee.

Awake! awake! and, like the sun, disperse
   All mists that would usurp this day:
Where are thy palms, thy branches, and thy verse?
   Hosanna! heark! why doest thou stay?
            Arise! Arise!
And with His healing bloud anoint thine eyes,
   Thy inward eyes: His bloud will cure thy mind,
   Whose spittle only could restore the blind.

                          HENRY VAUGHAN

"**Sing ye to the Lord, for he hath triumphed gloriously.**"

———

At the Lamb's high feast we sing
Praise to our victorious King,
Who hath washed us in the tide
Flowing from His piercèd side :
Praise we Him, whose love divine
Gives His sacred blood for wine,
Gives His body for the feast, —
Christ the Victim, Christ the Priest.

Where the Paschal blood is poured,
Death's dark angel sheathes his sword ;
Israel's hosts triumphant go
Through the wave that drowns the foe.
Praise we Christ whose blood was shed,
Paschal Victim, Paschal Bread ;
With sincerity and love
Eat we manna from above.

Mighty Victim from the sky!
Hell's fierce powers beneath Thee lie;
Thou hast conquered in the fight,
Thou hast brought us life and light:
Now no more can death appall,
Now no more the grave inthrall;
Thou hast opened Paradise,
And in Thee Thy saints shall rise.

Easter triumph, Easter joy,
Sin alone can this destroy;
From sin's power do Thou set free
Souls new-born, O Lord! in Thee.
Hymns of glory and of praise,
Risen Lord, to Thee we raise;
Holy Father, praise to Thee,
With the Spirit, ever be!

Translated by R. CAMPBELL.

"𝕳𝖊 𝖎𝖘 𝖗𝖎𝖘𝖊𝖓 : 𝖍𝖊 𝖎𝖘 𝖓𝖔𝖙 𝖍𝖊𝖗𝖊."

JESUS CHRIST is risen to-day, —
Our triumphant holy day, —
Who did once upon the cross
Suffer to redeem our loss.
                Hallelujah !

Hymns of praise then let us sing
Unto Christ our heavenly King,
Who endured the cross and grave,
Sinners to redeem and save.
                Hallelujah !

But the pains which He endured
Our salvation have procured ;
Now above the sky He's King,
Where the angels ever sing, —
                Hallelujah !

                      OLD LATIN HYMN.

"King of kings, and Lord of lords."

Christ the Lord is risen again ;
Christ hath broken every chain :
Hark ! angelic voices cry,
Singing ever more on high, —
    Alleluia !

He who gave for us His life,
Who for us endured the strife,
Is our Paschal Lamb to-day ;
We, too, sing for joy, and say, —
    Alleluia !

He who bore all pain and loss,
Comfortless upon the cross,
Lives in glory now on high,
Pleads for us, and hears our cry.
    Alleluia !

He who slumbered in the grave
Is exalted now to save;
Now through Christendom it rings,
That the Lamb is King of kings.
                Alleluia!

Now he bids us tell abroad
How the lost may be restored,
How the penitent forgiven,
How we, too, may enter heaven.
                Alleluia!

Thou, our Paschal Lamb indeed,
Christ, Thy ransomed people feed!
Take our sins and guilt away,
Let us sing by night and day, —
                Alleluia!

Translated by C. WINKWORTH.

"He will swallow up death in victory."

Hallelujah! Hallelujah!
Finished is the battle now;
The crown is on the Victor's brow!
    Hence with sadness!
    Sing with gladness, —
      Hallelujah!

Hallelujah! Hallelujah!
After sharp death that Him befell,
Jesus Christ hath conquered hell.
    Earth is singing,
    Heaven is ringing, —
      Hallelujah!

Hallelujah! Hallelujah!
On the third morning he arose,
Bright with victory o'er His foes.
    Sing we lauding
    And applauding, —
      Hallelujah!

Hallelujah! Hallelujah!
He hath closed hell's brazen door,
And heaven is open evermore!
    Hence with sadness!
    Sing with gladness, —
        Hallelujah!

Hallelujah! Hallelujah!
Lord, by Thy wounds we call on Thee,
So from ill death to set us free,
    That our living
    Be thanksgiving:
        Hallelujah!

FROM A LATIN HYMN.

"*The Lord hath done great things for us, whereof we are glad.*"

Come, ye faithful, raise the strain
   Of triumphant gladness!
God hath brought His Israel
   Into joy from sadness;
Loosed from Pharaoh's bitter yoke
   Jacob's sons and daughters;
Led them with unmoistened foot
   Through the Red Sea waters.

'Tis the spring of souls to-day:
   Christ hath burst His prison;
And, from three days' sleep in death,
   As a sun hath risen:
All the winter of our sins,
   Long and dark, is flying
From His light, to whom we give
   Laud and praise undying.

Now the queen of seasons, bright
    With the day of splendor,
With the royal feast of feasts,
    Comes its joy to render ;
Comes to glad Jerusalem,
    Who with true affection
Welcomes, in unwearied strains,
    Jesu's resurrection.

Neither might the gates of death,
    Nor the tomb's dark portal,
Nor the watchers, nor the seal,
    Hold thee as a mortal ;
But to-day amidst the twelve
    Thou didst stand bestowing
That thy peace, which evermore
    Passeth human knowing.

        FROM GREEK OF ST. JOHN OF DAMASCUS, 787.
                Translated by J. M. NEALE.

"Let us keep the feast, not with old leaven."

Purge we out the ancient leaven,
That the feast of earth and heaven
   We may celebrate aright;
On to-day our hope stands founded:
Moses teacheth how unbounded
   Is its virtue and its might.

This day Egypt's treasures spoiled,
And the Hebrews freed the toiled,
   Pressed with bondage and in chains;
From the mortar, brick, and stubble,
Heaviest toil and sorest trouble
   Had they known in Zoan's plains.

Now the voice of exultation,
Now the triumph of salvation,
   Free and wide its tidings flings:
This is the day the Lord hath made; the day
That bids our sin and sorrow flee away,
   Life and light and health that brings.

In the Law the types lay shaded;
In the promised end they faded, —
　　Christ, who all things consummates;
Christ, whose blood aside hath turned
That devouring sword which burned,
　　Waving wide, at Eden's gates.

Yea, that child, our mystic Laughter,
For whose sake the ram fell after,
　　Signifies the Joy of Life.
Joseph from the prison goeth:
Christ, by resurrection, showeth
　　He hath conquered in the strife.

He the Dragon that, devouring
Pharaoh's dragons, rose, o'erpowering
　　All their malice and their might;
He the Serpent set on high,
That the people might not die
　　From the fiery serpents' bite;

He the Hook that, hid awhile,
Pierced leviathan with guile;
　　He the Child that laid His hand
On the cockatrice's den,
That the ancient lord of men
　　Might avoid the ransomed land;

They, whose scorn the seer offended,
As to Bethel he ascended,
   Feel the bald-head's wrath, and flee;
David, after madness feigned,
Scapegoat now no more detained,
   Ritual sparrow — all go free;

Alien wedlock first despising,
With a jawbone, Samson, rising,
   Thousand Philistines hath slain;
Then, in Gaza as he tarried,
Forth her brazen gates he carried
   To the mountain from the plain;

Sleeping first the sleep of mortals,
Judah's Lion thus the portals
   Of the grave hath borne away:
While the Father's voice resounded,
He, with majesty unbounded,
   Sought our Mother's courts of day.

Jonah, by the tempest followed,
Whom the whale of old time swallowed,
Type of our true Jonah giving,
Three days past, is rendered living
   From that dark and narrow space.

Now the myrrh of Cyprus groweth,
Widelier spreadeth, sweetlier bloweth ;
Law its withered blossoms throweth,
    That the Church may take their place.

Death and Life have striven newly,
Jesus Christ hath risen truly ;
And with Christ ascended duly
    Many a witness that He lives.
Dawn of newness, happy morrow,
Wipes away our eve of sorrow ;
Since from death our life we borrow,
    Brightest joy the season gives.

Jesu, Victor, Life, and Head ;
Jesu, Way Thy people tread ;
By Thy death from death released,
Call us to the Paschal Feast,
    That with boldness we may come.
Living Water, Bread undying,
Vine, each branch with life supplying ;
Thou must cleanse us, Thou must feed us,
From the second death must lead us
    Upward to our Heavenly Home.

                    ADAM OF S. VICTOR.
                    Translated by J. M. NEALE.

"The day of Jesus Christ."

Rise, heart; thy Lord is risen. Sing His praise
               Without delays,
Who takes thee by the hand, that thou likewise
               With Him mayst rise;
That, as His death calcinèd thee to dust
His life may make thee gold, and, much more, just.

Awake, my lute, and struggle for thy part,
               With all thy art;
The cross taught all wood to resound His name,
               Who bore the same:
His stretchèd sinews taught all strings what key
·Is best to celebrate this most high day.

Consort, both heart and lute, and twist a song,
               Pleasant and long;
Or, since all music is but three parts vied,
               And multiplied,
Oh, let thy blessed Spirit bear a part,
And make up our defects with his sweet art.

I got me flowers to strew Thy way ;
  I got me boughs off many a tree ;
But Thou wast up by break of day,
  And brought'st Thy sweets along with thee.

The sun arising in the east,
  Though he gave light, and the east perfume,
If they should offer to contest
  With Thy arising, they presume.

Can there be any day but this,
  Though many suns to shine endeavor ?
We count three hundred, but we miss :
  There is but one, and that one ever.

GEORGE HERBERT.

"In Christ shall all be made alive."

Lord, who createdst man in wealth and store,
Though foolishly he lost the same,
Decaying more and more
Till he became
Most poor.

With Thee
O! let me rise
As larks, harmoniously,
And sing this day thy victories:
Then shall the fall further the flight in me.

My tender age in sorrow did begin;
And still with sicknesses and shame
Thou didst so punish sin,
That I became
Most thin.

With Thee
Let me combine,
And feel this day Thy victory;
For, if I imp my wing on Thine,
Affliction shall advance the flight in me.

GEORGE HERBERT.

"**Blessed are they that have not seen, and yet have believed.**"

O sons and daughters! let us sing!
The King of heaven, the glorious King,
O'er death to-day rose triumphing:
      Alleluia!

That Sunday morn, at break of day,
The faithful women went their way
To seek the tomb where Jesus lay.
      Alleluia!

An angel clad in white they see,
Who sat and spake unto the three, —
"Your Lord doth go to Galilee."
      Alleluia!

That night the apostles met in fear;
Amidst them came their Lord most dear,
And said, "My peace be on all here."
      Alleluia!

When Didymus the tidings heard,
He doubted if it were the Lord,
Until He came and spake this word : —
     Alleluia !

" My piercèd side, O Thomas ! see ;
My hands, my feet, I show to thee :
Nor faithless, but believing be."
     Alleluia !

No longer Thomas then denied ;
He saw the feet, the hands, the side :
" Thou art my Lord and God," he cried.
     Alleluia !

How blest are they who have not seen,
And yet whose faith has constant been !
For they eternal life shall win.
     Alleluia !

On this most holy day of days,
To God your hearts and voices raise
In laud, and jubilee, and praise !
     Alleluia ! Amen.
    HYMNS ANCIENT AND MODERN.

"Abide with us."

Light's glittering morn bedecks the sky,
Heaven thunders forth its victor-cry,
The glad earth shouts her triumph high,
And groaning hell makes wild reply;

While He, the King, the mighty King,
Despoiling death of all its sting,
And trampling down the powers of night,
Brings forth His ransomed saints to light.

His tomb of late the threefold guard
Of watch and stone and seal had barred;
But now, in pomp and triumph high,
He comes from death to victory.

The pains of hell are loosed at last;
The days of mourning now are past;
An angel robed in light hath said, —
"The Lord is risen from the dead."

The apostles' hearts were full of pain
For their dear Lord so lately slain,
By rebel servants doomed to die
A death of cruel agony.

With gentle voice the angel gave
The women tidings at the grave, —
"Fear not, your Master shall ye see:
He goes before to Galilee."

Then hastening on their eager way,
The joyful tidings to convey,
Their Lord they met, their living Lord,
And falling at His feet adored.

Th' eleven, when they hear, with speed
To Galilee forthwith proceed,
That there once more they may behold
The Lord's dear face as He foretold.

That Easter-tide with joy was bright,
The sun shone out with fairer light,
When, to their longing eyes restored,
The apostles saw their risen Lord.

He bade them see His hands, His side,
Where yet the glorious wounds abide, —
O tokens true! which made it plain
Their Lord indeed was risen again.

Jesu, the King of gentleness,
Do Thou Thyself our hearts possess,
That we may give Thee, all our days,
The tribute of our grateful praise.

O Lord of all! with us abide
In this our joyful Easter-tide:
From every weapon death can wield
Thine own redeemed forever shield.

All praise be Thine, O risen Lord,
From death to endless life restored!
All praise to God the Father be,
And Holy Ghost, eternally!

Hymns Ancient and Modern.

"Through death he might destroy him that had the power of death."

In the bonds of Death He lay,
    Who for our offence was slain;
But the Lord is risen to-day,
    Christ hath brought us life again.
Wherefore let us all rejoice,
Singing loud with cheerful voice, —
        Hallelujah!

Of the sons of men was none
    Who could break the bonds of Death;
Sin this mischief dire had done;
    Innocent was none on earth:
Wherefore Death grew strong and bold;
Death would all men captive hold.
        Hallelujah!

Jesus Christ, God's only Son,
    Came at last our woe to smite.
All our sins away hath done,
    Done away Death's power and right.
But the form of Death is left:
Of his sting he is bereft.
              Hallelujah!

'Twas a wondrous war, I trow,
    When Life and Death together fought;
Life hath triumphed o'er his foe,
    Death is mocked and set at nought;
Yea, 'tis as the Scripture saith,
Christ through death has conquered Death.
              Hallelujah!

Now our Paschal Lamb is He,
    And by Him alone we live,
Who, to death upon the tree,
    For our sakes Himself did give.
Faith His blood strikes on our door:
Death dares never harm us more.
              Hallelujah!

On this day, most blest of days,
    Let us keep high festival ;
For our God hath showed His grace,
    And our Sun hath risen on all ;
And our hearts rejoice to see
Sin and night before Him flee.
              Hallelujah !

To the supper of the Lord
    Gladly will we come to-day ;
The word of peace is now restored,
    The old leaven is put away.
Christ will be our food alone,
Faith no life but His doth own.
              Hallelujah !

LUTHER.

"Jesus met them, saying, All hail."

The day of resurrection!
    Earth, tell it out abroad!
The Passover of gladness,
    The Passover of God!
From death to life eternal,
    From this world to the sky,
Our Christ hath brought us over,
    With hymns of victory.

Our hearts be pure from evil,
    That we may see aright
The Lord in rays eternal
    Of resurrection light;
And, listening to His accents,
    May hear, so calm and plain,
His own "All hail!" and, hearing,
    May raise the victor-strain.

Now let the heavens be joyful,
    Let earth her song begin,
Let the round world keep triumph,
    And all that is therein!
Invisible and visible,
    Their notes let all things blend,
For Christ the Lord hath risen,
    Our joy that hath no end!

St. John of Damascus.
Translated by J. M. Neale.

"Lo, I am with you alway."

O GLORIOUS Head, Thou livest now!
    Let us Thy members share Thy life;
Canst Thou behold their need, nor bow
    To raise Thy children from the strife
With self and sin, with death and dark distress,
That they may live to Thee in holiness?

Earth knows Thee not, but evermore
    Thou liv'st in Paradise, in peace;
Thither my soul would also soar,
    Let me from the creatures cease;
Dead to the world, but to Thy Spirit known,
I live to Thee, O Prince of Life, alone.

Break through my bonds, whate'er it cost;
    What is not Thine within me slay;
Give me the lot I covet most, —
    To rise as Thou hast risen to-day.
Nought can I do, a slave to death I pine:
Work Thou in me, O Power and Life divine!

Work Thou in me, and heavenward guide
  My thoughts and wishes, that my heart
Waver no more, nor turn aside,
  But fix forever where Thou art.
Thou art not far from us : who loves Thee well,
While yet on earth, in heaven with Thee may dwell.

TERSTEEGEN.

"To him be glory both now and forever."

Hail, day of days! in peals of praise
   Throughout all ages owned,
When Christ, our God, hell's empire trod,
   And high o'er heaven was throned.

This glorious morn the world new-born
   In rising beauty shows;
How, with her Lord to life restored,
   Her gifts and graces rose!

The spring serene, in sparkling sheen,
   The flower-clad earth arrays;
Heaven's portal bright its radiant light
   In fuller flood displays.

The fiery sun in loftier noon
   O'er heaven's high orbit shines,
As o'er the tide of waters wide
   He rises and declines.

From hell's deep gloom, from earth's dark tomb,
    The Lord in triumph soars ;
The forests raise their leafy praise ;
    The flowery field adores.

As star by star He mounts afar,
    And hell imprisoned lies,
Let stars and light and depth and height
    In hallelujahs rise.

Lo ! He who died, the Crucified,
    God over all He reigns ;
On Him we call, His creatures all,
    Who heaven and earth sustains.

From the Latin of VENANTIUS FORTUNATUS.

"He appeared first to Mary Magdalene."

STILL thy sorrow, Magdalena!
   Wipe the tear-drops from thine eyes.
Not at Simon's board thou kneelest,
   Pouring thy repentant sighs:
All with thy glad heart rejoices;
All things sing with happy voices, —
      Hallelujah!

Laugh with rapture, Magdalena!
   Be thy drooping forehead bright;
Banished now is every anguish,
   Breaks anew thy morning light;
Christ from death the world hath freed:
He is risen, is risen indeed.
      Hallelujah!

Joy! exult, O Magdalena!
　He hath burst the rocky prison;
Ended are the days of darkness;
　Conqueror hath He arisen.
Mourn no more the Christ departed:
Run to welcome Him, glad hearted.
　　　Hallelujah!

Lift thine eyes, O Magdalena!
　See! thy living Master stands;
See His face, as ever, smiling;
　See those wounds upon His hands,
On His feet, His sacred side, —
Gems that deck the Glorified, —
　　　Hallelujah!

Live, now live, O Magdalena!
　Shining is thy new-born day;
Let thy bosom pant with pleasure,
　Death's poor terror flee away;
Far from thee the tears of sadness,
Welcome love and welcome gladness!
　　　Hallelujah!

　　　　　　　　From the Latin.
　　　　　　　Trans. by Dr. Washburn.

"𝔍 am he that liveth and was dead."

CHRIST the Lord is risen to-day,
Christians, haste your vows to pay:
Offer ye your praises meet
At the Paschal Victim's feet.
For the sheep the Lamb hath bled,
Sinless in the sinner's stead;
"Christ is risen," to-day we cry;
Now he lives no more to die.

Christ, the Victim undefiled,
Man to God hath reconciled,
Whilst in strange and awful strife
Met together death and life.
Christians, on this happy day,
Haste with joy your vows to pay:
"Christ is risen," to-day we cry;
Now he lives no more to die.

Christ, who once for sinners bled,
Now the first-born from the dead,
Throned in endless might and power,
Lives and reigns for evermore.
Hail, eternal Hope on high !
Hail, Thou King of victory !
Hail, Thou Prince of Life adored !
Help and save us, gracious Lord !
Hymns Ancient and Modern.

"Destroy this temple, and in three days I will
raise it up."

Blest morning, whose young dawning rays
   Beheld our rising God!
That saw Him triumph o'er the dust,
   And leave His dark abode.

In the cold prison of a tomb
   The dead Redeemer lay,
Till the revolving skies had brought
   The third, th' appointed day.

Hell and the grave unite their force
   To hold our God, in vain;
The sleeping Conqueror arose,
   And burst their feeble chain.

To Thy great name, Almighty Lord,
    These sacred hours we pay ;
And loud hosannas shall proclaim
    The triumph of the day.

Salvation and immortal praise
    To our victorious King!
Let heaven and earth, and rocks and seas,
    With glad hosannas ring!

WATTS.

"Peace be unto you."

O RISEN Lord! O conquering King!
   O Life of all that live!
To-day that peace of Easter bring
   Which only Thou canst give.
      Once Death, our foe,
      Had laid thee low:
Now hast Thou rent his bonds in twain,
Now art Thou risen who once wast slain.

The power of Thy great majesty
   Bursts rocks and tombs away;
Thy victory raises us with Thee
   Into the glorious day;
      Now Satan's might
      And death's dark night
Have lost their power this blessed morn,
And we to higher life are born.

Oh that our hearts might inly know
    Thy victory over death,
And, gazing on Thy conflict, glow
    With eager, dauntless faith!
        Thy quenchless light,
        Thy glorious might,
Still comfortless and lonely leave
The soul that cannot yet believe.

Then break throughout our hard hearts Thy way,
    O Jesus, conquering King!
Kindle the lamp of faith to-day;
    Teach our faint hearts to sing
        For joy at length,
        That in Thy strength
We too may rise whom sin had slain,
And Thine eternal rest attain.

And, when our tears for sin o'erflow,
    Do Thou in love draw near,
The precious gift of peace bestow,
    Shine on us bright and clear;
        That so may we,
        O Christ, from Thee,
Drink in the life that cannot die,
And keep true Easter feasts on high.

Yes, let us truly know within
   Thy rising from the dead ;
And quit the grave of death and sin,
   And keep that gift, our Head,
     That Thou didst leave
     For all who cleave
To Thee through all this earthly strife:
So shall we enter into life.

          FROM THE GERMAN OF BOEHMER.
          Translated by C. WINKWORTH.

"Death is swallowed up in victory."

"Christ the Lord is risen to-day,"
Sons of men, and angels, say:
Raise your joys and triumphs high;
Sing, ye heavens, and earth reply.

Love's redeeming work is done,
Fought the fight, the battle won;
Lo! our Sun's eclipse is o'er:
Lo! He sets in blood no more.

Vain the stone, the watch, the seal:
Christ hath burst the gates of hell;
Death in vain forbids Him rise;
Christ hath opened Paradise.

Lives again our glorious King:
Where, O death! is now thy sting?
Once he died our souls to save:
Where thy victory, O grave?

Soar we now where Christ has led,
Following our exalted Head;
Made like Him, like Him we rise;
Ours the cross, the grave, the skies.

What though once we perished all,
Partners in our parents' fall?
Second life we all receive,
In our heavenly Adam live.

Risen with Him, we upward move;
Still we seek the things above,
Still pursue and kiss the Son,
Seated on His Father's throne.

Scarce on earth a thought bestow,
Dead to all we leave below,
Heaven our aim and loved abode,
Hid our life with Christ in God,—

Hid, till Christ our life appear,
Glorious in His members here;
Joined to Him, we then shall shine,
All immortal, all divine.

Hail, the Lord of earth and heaven!
Praise to Thee by both be given!
Thee we greet triumphant now,
Hail, the Resurrection Thou!

King of glory, Soul of bliss!
Everlasting life is this,
Thee to know, Thy power to prove,
Thus to sing, and thus to love!

CHARLES WESLEY.

"Our Saviour, Jesus Christ, who hath abolished death,
and brought life and immortality to light
through the Gospel."

Welcome, Thou victor in the strife,
  Welcome from out the cave!
To-day we triumph in Thy life,
  Around Thine empty grave.

Our enemy is put to shame,
  His short-lived triumph o'er;
Our God is with us, we exclaim,
  We fear our foe no more.

The dwellings of the just resound
  With songs of victory;
For in their midst, Lord, Thou art found,
  And bringest peace with thee.

O share with us the spoils, we pray,
  Thou diedst to achieve;
We meet within Thy house to-day,
  Our portion to receive.

And let Thy conquering banner wave
    O'er hearts Thou makest free,
And point the path that from the grave
    Leads heavenward up to Thee.

We bury all our sin and crime
    Deep in our Saviour's tomb,
And seek the treasure there, that time
    Nor change can e'er consume.

We die with Thee: oh, let us live
    Henceforth to Thee aright!
The blessings Thou hast died to give
    Be daily in our sight.

Fearless we lay us in the tomb,
    And sleep the night away,
If Thou art there to break the gloom,
    And call us back to day.

Death hurts us not: his power is gone,
    And pointless all his darts;
Now hath God's favor on us shone,
    And joy fills all our hearts.

                    SCHMOLKE.
            Translated by C. WINKWORTH.

"If any man thirst, let him come unto me and drink."

Sun, shine forth in all thy splendor,
    Joyfully pursue thy way,
For thy Lord and my Defender
    Rose triumphant on this day.
When he bowed His head, sore troubled,
    Thou didst hide thyself in night:
Shine forth now with rays redoubled;
    He is risen who is thy light.

Earth, be joyous and glad-hearted,
    Spread out all thy vernal bloom;
For thy Lord is not departed,
    He has broken through the tomb.
When the Lord expired, wide yawning
    Thy strong rocks were rent with fright:
Greet thy risen Lord this morning,
    Bathed in floods of rosy light.

Say, my soul, what preparation
    Makest thou for this high day,
When the God of thy salvation
    Opened through the tomb a way?
Dwellest thou with pure affection
    On this proof of power and love?
Doth thy Saviour's resurrection
    Raise thy thoughts to things above?

Hast thou, borne on faith's strong pinion,
    Risen with the risen Lord!
And, released from sin's dominion,
    Into purer regions soared?
Or art thou, in spite of warning,
    Dead in trespasses and sin?
Hath to thee the purple morning
    No true Easter ushered in?

Oh, then, let not death o'ertake thee
    By the shades of night o'erspread:
See! thy Lord has come to wake thee,
    He is risen from the dead.
While the time as yet allows thee,
    Hear; the gracious Saviour cries, —
"Sleeper, from thy sloth arouse thee,
    To new life at once arise!"

See, with looks of tender pity
   He extends His wounded hands,
Bidding thee with fond entreaty,
   Shake off sin's inthralling bands:
"Wait not for some future meetness,
   Dread no punishment from Me:
Rouse thyself, and taste the sweetness
   Of the new life offered thee."

Let no precious time be wasted,
   To new life arise at length,
He who death for thee hath tasted,
   For new life will give new strength.
Try to rise; at once bestir thee,
   Still press on and persevere,
Let no weariness deter thee:
   He who woke thee still is near.

Waste not so much time in weighing
   When and where thou shalt begin:
Too much thinking is delaying,
   Rivets but the chains of sin.
He will help thee, and provide thee
   With a courage not thine own,
Bear thee in His arms, and guide thee,
   Till thou learn'st to walk alone.

See! thy Lord Himself is risen,
　That thou mightest also rise,
And emerge from sin's dark prison
　To new life and open skies.
Come to Him, who can unbind thee,
　And reverse thy awful doom;
Come to Him, and leave behind thee
　Thy old life — an empty tomb.

Lyra Domestica.

"He is risen from the dead."

"The Lord is risen indeed;"
   Then hell has lost his prey:
With Him is risen the ransomed seed
   To reign in endless day.

"The Lord is risen indeed;"
   He lives to die no more;
He lives the sinner's cause to plead,
   Whose curse and shame He bore.

"The Lord is risen indeed;"
   Attending angels, hear:
Up to the courts of heaven, with speed,
   The joyful tidings bear.

Then take your golden lyres,
   And strike each cheerful chord;
Join all the bright celestial choirs,
   To sing our risen Lord.

KELLY.

"I know that my Redeemer liveth."

Jesus lives : no longer now
    Can thy terrors, Death, appall us :
Jesus lives : by this we know
    Thou, O grave ! canst not inthrall us.
                   Alleluia !

Jesus lives : henceforth is death
    But the gate of life immortal ;
This shall calm our trembling breath,
    When we pass its gloomy portal.
                   Alleluia !

Jesus lives : for us He died :
    Then, alone to Jesus living,
Pure in heart may we abide,
    Glory to our Saviour giving.
                   Alleluia !

Jesus lives : our hearts know well
    Nought from us His love shall sever ;
Life, nor death, nor powers of hell
    Tear us from His keeping ever.
                      Alleluia !

Jesus lives : to Him the throne
    Over all the world is given :
May we go where He is gone,
    Rest and reign with Him in heaven.
                      Alleluia !
                      C. F. GELLERT.

"𝕮𝖍𝖗𝖎𝖘𝖙 must needs have suffered, and risen again from the dead."

Yes, the Redeemer rose ;
  The Saviour left the dead,
And o'er our hellish foes
  High raised His conquering head.
    In wild dismay,
    The guards around
    Fell to the ground,
    And sunk away.

Lo ! the angelic bands
  In full assembly meet,
To wait His high commands,
  And worship at His feet ;
    Joyful they come,
    And wing their way
    From realms of day
    To such a tomb.

Then back to heaven they fly,
   And the glad tidings bear;
Hark! as they soar on high,
   What music fills the air!
      Their anthems say,—
      "Jesus, who bled,
      Hath left the dead;
      He rose to-day."

Ye mortals, catch the sound,
   Redeemed by Him from hell,
And send the echo round
   The globe on which you dwell;
      Transported cry,—
      "Jesus, who bled,
      Hath left the dead,
      No more to die."

All hail, triumphant Lord,
   Who sav'st us with Thy blood!
Wide be Thy name adored,
   Thou rising, reigning God!
      With Thee we rise,
      With Thee we reign,
      And empires gain
      Beyond the skies.
                        DODDRIDGE.

"Why weepest thou? Whom seekest thou?"

A PATHWAY opens from the tomb,
    The grave's a grave no more!
Stoop down : look into that sweet room,
    Pass through the unsealed door;
Linger a moment by the bed,
Where lay but yesterday the Church's Head.

What is there there to make thee fear?
    A folded chamber-vest,
Akin to that which thou shalt wear
    When for thy slumber drest;
Two gentle angels sitting by, —
How sweet a room, methinks, wherein to lie!

No gloomy vault, no charnel cell,
    No emblems of decay,
No solemn sound of passing-bell,
    To say, "He's gone away;"
But angel-whispers soft and clear,
And He, the risen Jesus, standing near.

"Why weepest thou? Whom seekest thou?"
    'Tis not the gardener's voice,
But His to whom all knees shall bow,
    In whom all hearts rejoice;
The voice of Him who yesterday
Within that rock was Death's resistless prey.

"Why weepest thou? Whom seekest thou?
    The living with the dead?"
Take young spring flowers, and deck thy brow,
    For life with joy is wed:
The grave is now the grave no more;
Why fear to pass that bridal chamber door?

Take flowers, and strew them all around
    The room where Jesus lay:
But softly tread; 'tis hallowed ground,
    And this is Easter Day.
"The Lord is risen," as He said,
And thou shalt rise with Him, thy risen Head.

                        LYRA ANGLICANA.

"I will see you again, and your heart shall rejoice, and your joy no man taketh from you."

As spring's sweet breath after long wintry snow,
   As land to voyager o'er pathless sea,
As daybreak after weary night of woe,
   Is Easter joy to me.

All Lenten shadows over, and the light
   Around us and within so sweet and strong!
Teach us, O risen Master, how aright
   To sing our Easter song.

We stand to-day beside Thy open tomb,
   We gaze on "linen clothes" with reverent heed,
And hear the angels whispering thro' the gloom, —
   "Not here but risen indeed!"

And all the story of Thy love divine
   Throbs through our hearts, longing, O Christ, for Thee!
The bitter chalice with the deadly wine
   Was drained to set us free.

The grave is dark no more: a stream of light
    He, rising, left behind for all His own:
Death's chain is broken by His arm of might,
    And rolled away the stone.

Now Easter light flushes the morning sky;
    Thy form we see, all changed and yet the same.
Master! we kneel before Thee; hear our cry,
    And call us each by name.

When evening shadows lengthen all around,
    And we to Emmaus take our weary way,
With us, O risen Saviour, still be found,
    And turn our night to day.

And, from Thy radiant throne of light above,
    Oh, send us, till our desert wanderings cease,
Thine own best legacy of tender love, —
    Thy sweetest gift of peace!

Then at the last, when all shall wake who sleep,
    Made like to Thee, in raiment white and fair,
Oh, bid us welcome to Thy home, to keep
    Our endless Easter there!

                        R. H. BAYNES.

"**Bless the Lord, O my soul: and all that is within me, bless his holy name.**"

AGAIN the Lord of life and light
    Awakes the kindling ray,
Unseals the eyelids of the morn,
    And pours increasing day.

Oh, what a night was that which wrapped
    The heathen world in gloom!
Oh, what a sun which broke this day
    Triumphant from the tomb!

This day be grateful homage paid,
    And loud hosannas sung;
Let gladness dwell in every heart,
    And praise on every tongue.

Ten thousand differing lips shall join
    To hail this welcome morn,
Which scatters blessings from its wings
    To nations yet unborn.

                    MRS. BARBAULD.

"Thou art worthy, O Lord, to receive glory and honor and power."

Come, ye saints, look here and wonder:
See the place where Jesus lay;
He has burst His bands asunder;
He has borne our sins away;
Joyful tidings!
Yes, the Lord has risen to-day.

Jesus triumphs! Sing ye praises:
By His death he overcame:
Thus the Lord His glory raises,
Thus He fills His foes with shame.
Sing ye praises,
Praises to the Victor's name.

Jesus triumphs! Countless legions
Come from heaven to meet their King;
Soon, in yonder blessed regions,
They shall join His praise to sing.
Songs eternal
Shall through heaven's high arches ring.

T. Kelly.

"In my Father's house are many mansions."

Do saints keep holy-day in heavenly places?
Does the old joy shine new in angel faces?
Are hymns still sung the night when Christ was born,
And anthems on the resurrection morn?

Because our little year of earth is run,
Do they make record there beyond the sun?
And, in their homes of light so far away,
Mark with us the sweet coming of this day?

What is their Easter? For they have no graves;
No shadow there the holy sunrise craves,
Deep in the heart of noontide marvellous,
Whose breaking glory reaches down to us.

How did the Lord keep Easter? With His own!
Back to meet Mary where she grieved alone;
With face and mien all tenderly the same,
Unto the very sepulchre He came.

Ah, the dear message that He gave her then,
Said for the sake of all bruised hearts of men! —
"Go, tell those friends who have believed on Me,
I go before them into Galilee.

Into the life so poor and hard and plain,
That for a while they must take up again,
My presence passes. Where their feet toil slow,
Mine, shining swift with love, still foremost go.

Say, Mary, I will meet them: by the way,
To walk a little with them; where they stay,
To bring My peace. Watch! for ye do not know
The day, the hour, when I may find you so."

And I do think, as He came back to her,
The many mansions may be all astir
With tender steps that hasten in the way,
Seeking their own upon this Easter Day.

Parting the veil that hideth them about,
I think they do come, softly wistful, out
From homes of Heaven that only *seem* so far,
And walk in gardens where the new tombs are.

A. D. T. WHITNEY.

"**They found the stone rolled away from the sepulchre.**"

MORNING breaks upon the tomb;
Jesus dissipates its gloom;
Day of triumph through the skies,
See the glorious Saviour rise!

Christians, dry your flowing tears;
Chase those unbelieving fears;
Look on His deserted grave:
Doubt no more His power to save.

Ye who are of death afraid,
Triumph in the scattered shade;
Drive your anxious fears away,
See the place where Jesus lay.

So the rising sun appears,
Shedding radiance o'er the spheres;
So returning beams of light
Chase the terrors of the night.

COLLYER.

"**Ho, every one that thirsteth, come ye to the waters.**"

I SAY to all men, far and near,
    That He is risen again:
That He is with us now and here,
    And ever shall remain.

And, what I say, let each this morn
    Go tell it to his friend,
That soon in every place shall dawn
    His kingdom without end.

Now first to souls who thus awake
    Seems earth a fatherland:
A new and endless life they take,
    With rapture from His hand.

The fears of death and of the grave
    Are whelmed beneath the sea;
And every heart now light and brave
    May face the things to be.

The way of darkness that He trod
  To heaven at last shall come ;
And he who hearkens to His word
  Shall reach his Father's home.

Now let the mourner grieve no more,
  Though his beloved sleep ;
A happier meeting shall restore
  Their light to eyes that weep.

Now every heart each noble deed
  With new resolve may dare ;
A glorious harvest shall the seed
  In happier regions bear.

He lives: His presence hath not ceased,
  Though foes and fears be rife ;
And thus we hail, in Easter's feast,
  A world renewed to life.

From the German.

"Weeping may endure for a night, but joy cometh in the morning."

MARY, to her Saviour's tomb,
  Hasted at the early dawn:
Spice she brought, and sweet perfume,
  But the Lord she loved was gone.
For a while she weeping stood,
  Struck with horror and surprise,
Shedding tears, a plenteous flood,
  For her heart supplied her eyes.

Grief and sighing quickly fled
  When she heard His welcome voice;
Just before she thought Him dead:
  Now He bids her heart rejoice.
What a change His word can make,
  Turning darkness into day!
You who weep for Jesus' sake,
  He will wipe your tears away.

He who came to comfort her
    When she thought her all was lost,
Will for your relief appear,
    Though you now are tempest-tossed.
On His word your burden cast,
    On His love your thoughts employ:
Weeping for a while may last,
    But the morning brings the joy.

JOHN NEWTON.

"He is not here, but is risen."

Oh, day of days! shall hearts set free
No "minstrel rapture" find for thee?
Thou art the Sun of other days:
They shine by giving back thy rays.

Enthronèd in thy sovereign sphere,
Thou shedd'st thy light on all the year;
Sundays by thee more glorious break,
An Easter Day in every week;

And weekdays, following in their train,
The fulness of thy blessing gain,
Till all, both resting and employ,
Be one Lord's day of holy joy.

Then wake, my soul, to high desires,
And earlier light thine altar fires:
The World some hours is on her way,
Nor thinks on thee, thou blessed day;

Or, if she think, it is in scorn;
The vernal light of Easter morn
To her dark gaze no brighter seems
Than reason's or the law's pale beams.

"Where is your Lord?" she scornful asks:
"Where is His hire? we know His tasks;
Sons of a King ye boast to be:
Let us your crowns and treasures see."

We in the words of truth reply,
(An angel brought them from the sky), —
"Our crown, our treasure, is not here:
'Tis stored above the highest sphere.

Methinks your wisdom guides amiss,
To seek on earth a Christian's bliss;
We watch not now the lifeless stone:
Our only Lord is risen and gone."

Yet even the lifeless stone is dear
For thoughts of Him who late lay here;
And the base world, now Christ hath died,
Ennobled is and glorified.

No more a charnel-house to fence
The relics of lost innocence, —
A vault of ruin and decay;—
Th' imprisoning stone is rolled away.

'Tis now a cell, where angels use
To come and go with heavenly news,
And in the ears of mourners say, —
"Come, see the place where Jesus lay."

'Tis now a fane where Love can find
Christ everywhere embalmed and shrined;
Aye gathering up memorials sweet,
Where'er she sets her duteous feet.

Oh, joy to Mary first allowed,
When roused from weeping o'er His shroud,
By His own calm, soul-soothing tone,
Breathing her name as still His own!

Joy to the faithful three renewed,
As their glad errand they pursued!
Happy, who so Christ's word convey,
That He may meet them on their way!

So is it still : to holy tears,
In lonely hours, Christ risen appears :
In social hours, who Christ would see
Must turn all tasks to charity.

                                      J. KEBLE.

"O death, where is thy sting? O grave, where is
thy victory?"

Angel, roll the stone away!
Death, give up thy mighty prey!
See! He rises from the tomb,
Glowing in immortal bloom.

Shout, ye saints, in rapturous song ;
Let the notes be sweet and strong :
Hail the Son of God, this morn,
From His sepulchre new-born !

Christians, dry your flowing tears ;
Calm those unbelieving fears ;
Doubt no more His power to save :
See His own deserted grave !

Powers of heaven, celestial choirs,
Sing and sweep your sounding lyres ;
Sons of men, in joyful strain
Hail your mighty Saviour's reign.

Every note with rapture swell,
And the Saviour's triumph tell:
Where, O death, is now thy sting?
Where, thy terrors, vanquished king?

J. Scott.

"O clap your hands, all ye people: shout unto God with the voice of triumph."

Lift your glad voices in triumph on high,
For Jesus hath risen, and man cannot die.
Vain were the terrors that gathered around Him,
   And short the dominion of death and the grave;
He burst from the fetters of darkness that bound Him,
   Resplendent in glory, to live and to save.
Loud was the chorus of angels on high, —
"The Saviour hath risen, and man shall not die."

Glory to God, in full anthems of joy!
The being He gave us death cannot destroy.
Sad were the life we must part with to-morrow,
   If tears were our birthright, and death were our end;
But Jesus hath cheered the dark valley of sorrow,
   And bade us immortal to Heaven ascend.
Lift, then, your glad voices in triumph on high,
For Jesus hath risen, and man shall not die.

                              Henry Ware.

"The first-begotten of the dead."

COME see the place where Jesus lay,
And hear angelic watchers say, —
  "He lives, who once was slain:
Why seek the living 'midst the dead?
Remember how the Saviour said
  That He would rise again."

Oh, joyful sound! Oh, glorious hour,
When by His own almighty power
  He rose and left the grave!
Now let our songs His triumph tell,
Who burst the bands of death and hell,
  And ever lives to save.

The First-begotten of the dead,
For us He rose, our glorious Head,
  Immortal life to bring;
What though the saints like Him shall die?
They share their Leader's victory,
  And triumph with their King.

No more they tremble at the grave,
For Jesus will their spirits save,
  And raise their slumbering dust;
O risen Lord, in Thee we live:
To Thee our ransomed souls we give,
  To Thee our bodies trust.

T. S. KELLY.

"It is Christ that died, yea, rather, that is risen again."

He is risen! He is risen!
  Tell it with a joyful voice:
He has burst His three-days' prison;
  Let the whole wide earth rejoice;
Death is vanquished, man is free:
Christ has won the victory.

Tell it to the sinners, weeping
  Over deeds in darkness done,
Weary fast and vigil keeping,—
  Brightly breaks their Easter sun:
Christ has borne our sins away,
Christ has conquered hell to-day.

He is risen! He is risen!
  He has oped the eternal gate:
We are loosed from sin's dark prison,
  Risen to a holier state,
Where a brightening Easter beam
On our longing eyes shall stream.

C. F. ALEXANDER.

"Jesus Christ, the Lord of glory."

The strife is o'er, the battle done ;
The victory of life is won :
The song of triumph has begun :
                Hallelujah !

The powers of death have done their worst,
But Christ their legions hath dispersed ;
Let shout of holy joy outburst :
                Hallelujah !

The three sad days are quickly sped ;
He rises glorious from the dead ;
All glory to our risen Head !
                Hallelujah !

He closed the yawning gates of hell ;
The bars from heaven's high portals fell ;
Let hymns of praise His triumphs tell :
                Hallelujah !

Lord, by the stripes which wounded Thee,
From death's dread sting Thy servants free,
That we may live and sing to Thee,
              Hallelujah!

F. Pott.

"The fruit of the Spirit is in all goodness and righteousness and truth."

How shall we keep this holy day of gladness,
This queen of days, that bitter, hopeless sadness
    Forever drives away?
The night is past, — its sleep and its forgetting:
Our risen sun, no more forever setting,
    Pours everlasting day.

Let us not bring, upon this joyful morning,
Dead myrrh and spices for our Lord's adorning,
    Nor any lifeless thing:
Our gift shall be the fragrance and the splendor
Of living flowers, in breathing beauty tender,
    The glory of our spring.

And, with the myrrh, oh, put away the leaven
Of malice, hatred, injuries unforgiven,
    And cold and lifeless form;
Still, with the lilies, deeds of mercy bringing,
And fervent prayers, and praises upward springing,
    And hopes pure, bright, and warm.

So shall this Easter shed a fragrant beauty
O'er many a day of dull and cheerless duty,
    And light thy wintry way;
Till rest is won, and patience, smiling faintly,
Upon thy breast shall lay her lilies saintly,
    To hail heaven's Easter Day.

E. S.

"To the only wise God, our Saviour, be glory and majesty, dominion and power, both now and ever. Amen."

OUR Lord is risen to-day!
How glad th' angelic lay
    Resoundeth "Hallelujah!"
Men too, with feebler song,
That heavenly strain prolong,
    Repeating "Hallelujah!"
Through darkest realms of woe,
Sweet notes of mercy go,
    Re-echoing "Hallelujah!"
Let every living thing
Therefore break forth and sing,
    Exultant, "Hallelujah!"

Death quenched not Light of light:
He, clad in matchless might,
    To deepest hell descended.
He preached to spirits there;
And, at His word, despair
    And death and pain are ended.
Out through the gates of brass
The new-born armies pass;
    While saints, in raptured chorus,
Behold that host draw nigh,
And loud "Hosanna!" cry,—
    "All hail, Thou King victorious!"

Before the dawning's birth,
Up to the waiting earth
    Our Jesus swift returneth.
Through that same stone He rose,
Fast sealèd by His foes:
    Their malice thus He scorneth.
Earth quaked with fear and dread,
And Roman soldiers fled,
    When, clad in radiance splendid,
One heavenly hand alone
Rolled back the mighty stone,
    And Death's short victory ended!

Now shining angels tell
How bands of earth and hell
    By Him were burst in sunder.
With spices in their hand,
Lo! holy women stand,
    And list in thrilling wonder:
Then, trembling with the joy,
Unto the eleven they fly,
    That *men* also may greet Him:
"The Lord is risen," they say,
"The Lord is risen to-day:
    Oh, go ye forth to meet Him!"

Ascend Thy conquering car,
Thou mighty Man of War,
    With all Thy saints surrounded!
Shine forth in perfect day,
And let Thy loving sway
    Spread far o'er realms unbounded:
Till to the lower world
Thy deadly foes are hurled, —
    Cast down, to rise up never;
And Thou, Immanuel,
O'er heaven and earth and hell
    Triumphant reign forever!

To God the Father, Son,
And Spirit, Three in One,
    Eternal praise be given,
By all of mortal birth
Within the Church on earth,
    And countless hosts of heaven:
As was on that bright morn
When heaven and earth were born,
    And songs of praise ascended;
Is now, and shall be so, —
Still swelling as they go, —
    When time itself is ended.

J. H. Hopkins, Jun.

"Christ, being raised from the dead, dieth no more."

ANGELS.

Christ hath arisen!
Joy to our buried Head!
Whom the unmerited,
Trailing inherited
   Woes, did imprison!

WOMEN.

Costly devices
   We had prepared, —
Shrouds and sweet spices,
   Linen and nard,
Woe the disaster!
   Whom we here laid,
Gone is the Master,
   Empty His bed.

ANGELS.

Christ hath arisen!
Loving and glorious,
Out of laborious
Conflict victorious,
　　Christ hath arisen.

DISCIPLES.

Hath the inhumated
　　Upward aspiring,
Hath He consummated
　　All His desiring?
Is He in being's bliss
　　Near to creative joy?
Wearily we in this
　　Earthly house sigh:
Empty and hollow, us
　　Left He unblest.
Master! Thy followers
　　Envy Thy rest.

ANGELS.

Christ hath arisen
  Out of corruption's womb.
Burst every prison!
  Vanish death's gloom!
Active in charity,
Praise Him in verity!
His feast prepare it ye!
His message bear it ye!
His joy declare it ye!
  Then is the Master near,
  Then is He here.

GOETHE.
Translated by F. H. HEDGE.

"**Why seek ye the living among the dead?**"

———

UNCHANGED, through all the changing years,
    The widowed Church at dawning gray
Goes forth to kneel beside the tomb
    Where once our Lord and Saviour lay;

And carries with her, spice and balm,
    That through the air their fragrance shed:
Oh, hush, nor ask of her in scorn, —
    "Why seek the living 'mid the dead?"

Draw near, and see her precious store
    Until she all her gifts display,
Which all the year she garners up,
    And pours them forth on Easter Day.

And first, she brings her children's prayers,
    Which she has taught them day by day
Through life and death to offer still
    At home, at sea, or far away.

And next she gives each loving word,
    And every holy fruitful thought,
Each effort for the souls of men,
    Each work in love and mercy wrought;

And then her last and choicest gift
    Wherewith she crowneth all the rest, —
The memory of her holy dead
    Who sleep, of perfect peace possessed.

Still bears she forth her precious hoard,
    And hope grows strong with every year,
That many Easters shall not pass
    Before her Bridegroom shall appear.

Then shall her days of fasting end,
    And she her weeds aside will lay;
For Death and Sin shall be no more
    When dawns that endless Easter Day!

E. S.

"Alleluia, for the Lord God Omnipotent reigneth."

THE Lord of life is risen!
  Sing, Easter heralds, sing!
He burst His rocky prison:
  Wide let the triumph ring.
Tell how the graves are quaking,
The saints their fetters breaking:
  Sing, heralds: Jesus lives!

In death no longer lying,
  He rose the Prince to-day:
Life of the dead and dying,
  He triumphed o'er decay.
The Lord of life is risen:
In ruins lies death's prison,
  Its keeper bound in chains.

We hear, in Thy blest greeting,
   Salvation's work is done!
We worship Thee, repeating,
   Life for the dead is won!
O Head of all believing!
O Joy of all the grieving!
   Unite us, Lord, to Thee.

Here at Thy tomb, O Jesus!
   How sweet the morning's breath!
We hear in all the breezes, —
   Where is thy sting, O Death?
Dark hell flies in commotion;
While, far o'er earth and ocean,
   Loud hallelujahs ring!

Oh, publish this salvation,
   Ye heralds, through the earth!
To every buried nation
   Proclaim the day of birth!
Till, rising from their slumbers,
The countless heathen numbers
   Shall hail the risen light.

Hail, hail, our Jesus risen!
    Sing, ransomed brethren, sing!
Through death's dark, gloomy prison,
    Let Easter chorals ring.
Haste, haste, ye captive legions!
Come forth from sin's dark regions:
    In Jesus' kingdom live.

FROM THE GERMAN.

"**Let every thing that hath breath praise the Lord.**"

LET the merry church-bells ring:
   Hence with tears and sighing:
Frost and cold have fled from spring;
   Life hath conquered dying;
Flowers are smiling, fields are gay,
   Sunny is the weather:
With our risen Lord to-day
   All things rise together.

Let the birds sing out again
   From their leafy chapel,
Praising Him with whom in vain
   Sin hath sought to grapple.
Sounds of joy come loud and clear
   As the breezes flutter:
"He arose, and is not here,"
   Is the strain they utter.

Let the past of grief be past :
    This our comfort giveth, —
He was slain on Friday last,
    But to-day He liveth :
Mourning hearts must needs be gay
    Out of sorrow's prison,
Since the very grave can say,
    " Christ — He hath arisen ! "

"The flowers appear on the earth; the time of the singing of birds has come."

Sweetly are the birds singing
    At Easter dawn ;
Sweetly are the bells ringing
    On Easter morn ;
And the words that they say
    On Easter Day
Are, Christ the Lord is risen !

Birds, forget not your singing
    At Easter dawn ;
Bells, may ye always be ringing
    On Easter morn.
In the spring of the year,
    When Easter is here,
Sing, Christ the Lord is risen !

Easter buds were growing
    Ages ago;
Easter lilies were blowing
    By the water's flow.
All nature was glad,
    Not a creature was sad,
For, Christ the Lord is risen!

Buds, ye will soon be flowers,
    Cherry and white;
Snow-storms are changing to showers,
    Darkness to light.
With the wakening of spring,
    Oh, sweetly sing,
Lo, Christ the Lord is risen!

E. D. C.
St. Nicholas Magazine.

"Very early in the morning, the first day of the week,
they came unto the sepulchre at the rising
of the sun."

THE world itself keeps Easter Day,
    And Easter larks are singing;
And Easter flowers are blooming gay,
    And Easter buds are springing.
The Lord of all things lives anew,
And all His works are rising too.
    Alleluia! Alleluia! Alleluia!
        Praise the Lord!

There stood three Marys by the tomb,
    On Easter morning early,
When day had scarcely chased the gloom,
    And dew was white and pearly:
With loving but with erring mind
They came, the Prince of Life to find.
    Alleluia! Alleluia! Alleluia!
        Praise the Lord!

But earlier still the angel sped,
    His words of comfort giving ;
"And why," he said, "among the dead,
    Thus seek ye for the living?"
The risen Jesus lives again,
To save the souls of sinful men.
    Alleluia! Alleluia! Alleluia!
        Praise the Lord!

The world itself keeps Easter Day,
    And Easter larks are singing ;
And Easter flowers are blooming gay,
    And Easter buds are springing.
The Lord is risen, as all things tell :
Good Christians, see ye rise as well.
    Alleluia! Alleluia! Alleluia!
        Praise the Lord!

"Them also which sleep in Jesus will God bring with him."

ALLELUIA! Alleluia!
  Hearts to heaven, and voices, raise;
Sing to God a hymn of gladness,
  Sing to God a hymn of praise.
He who, on the cross a victim,
  For the world's salvation bled,
Jesus Christ the King of glory,
  Now is risen from the dead.

Now the iron bars are broken:
  Christ from death to life is born,
Glorious life and life immortal,
  On this holy Easter morn.
Christ has triumphed, and we conquer
  By His mighty enterprise;
We, with Christ to life eternal,
  By His resurrection rise.

Christ is risen, Christ, the first-fruits
    Of the holy harvest field,
Which will all its full abundance
    At His second coming yield :
Then the golden ears of harvest
    Will their heads before Him wave,
Ripened by His glorious sunshine,
    From the furrows of the grave.

Christ is risen, we are risen:
    Shed upon us heavenly grace,
Rain and dew, and gleams of glory,
    From the brightness of Thy face;
That we, Lord, with hearts in heaven,
    Here on earth may fruitful be,
And by angel hands be gathered,
    And be ever safe with Thee.

Alleluia! Alleluia!
    Glory be to God on high,
To the Father, and the Saviour,
    Who has gained the victory.
Glory to the Holy Spirit,
    Fount of love and sanctity.
Alleluia! Alleluia!
    To the Triune Majesty!

CANTERBURY HYMNAL.

"This is the day which the Lord hath made. We will
rejoice and be glad in it."

This is the feast-day of our King
  Who reigns in heaven above, —
A day which should be dear to men,
  And which the angels love.
Accept, O glorious risen King,
  The homage that we pay:
Let it ascend the starry sphere,
  This happy Easter Day.

Sweet are the chants the church doth raise
  To greet her risen King,
But sweeter far the songs of praise,
  The happy angels sing.
And yet accept, O glorious King,
  The homage that we pay:
Let it ascend the starry sphere,
  This happy Easter Day.

Though bright the blossoms we have brought,
  Thy house to beautify,
What are they to the changeless flowers
  That ever bloom on high?
And yet accept, O glorious King,
  The homage that we pay :
Let it ascend the starry sphere,
  This happy Easter Day.

The sky is clear, and bright the sun,
  That sheds on us his ray ;
But, where Thy beauteous presence shines,
  There is eternal day.
Accept, O glorious risen King,
  The homage that we pay ;
Let it ascend the starry sphere,
  This happy Easter Day.

FROM ENGLISH BOOK OF HYMNS AND CAROLS.

"Your joy no man taketh from you."

Days grow longer, sunbeams stronger,
    Easter-tide makes all things new;
Lent is banished, sadness vanished,
    Christ hath risen, rise we too.

Christmas greetings, Twelfth-Night meetings,
    Whitsun sports are glad and gay;
But the lightest and the brightest
    Of our feasts is Easter Day.

Earthly story crowns with glory
    Him whom earthly foes o'ercame;
Victor's laurel ends the quarrel,
    Honor dwells about His name.

Vanquished legions, conquered regions,
    Kings deposed, and princes bound;
Exultation, acclamation,
    Fill His ears, and float around.

Then, unending and transcending
  Be the glory of the Son:
For transcendent and resplendent
  Was the victory he hath won.

Death hath yielded, life is shielded,
  Satan bound, and hell in chains;
Chased is terror, fled is error,
  Grief is past, and joy remains.

FROM ENGLISH BOOK OF HYMNS AND CAROLS.

"Arise, shine; for thy light is come, and the glory of the Lord is risen upon thee."

Christ is risen! Christ is risen!
  Oh, let the joyful sounds
Through every land re-echo,
  To earth's remotest bounds:
    Christ is risen! Christ is risen!

Christ is risen! Christ is risen!
  Bright angels join the cry:
Hallelujahs ever singing
  Before the throne on high.
    Christ is risen! Christ is risen!

Christ is risen! Christ is risen!
  Ere earliest morning ray,
Wake, slumbering hearts, awake! arise!
  And speed you on your way.
    Christ is risen! Christ is risen!

Christ is risen! Christ is risen!
   To all the words repeat,
Till every knee before Him bow
   In adoration meet.
       Christ is risen! Christ is risen!

Christ is risen! Christ is risen!
   Bid all His praises sing;
Praise Him, the God of earth and heaven,
   Redeemer, Lord, and King.
       Christ is risen! Christ is risen!

"When Christ, who is our life, shall appear, then shall
ye also appear with him in glory."

Hark! the angels bright are singing
In the glorious Easter sky;
Jesus from the grave has risen,
Jesus now no more may die.
Alleluia, alleluia, this is what the angels say:
Alleluia, alleluia, we will sing with them to-day.

In vain the soldiers tried to keep
The Holy One within the grave;
In vain they put a seal and stone
Upon the entrance to the cave.
Alleluia, alleluia, this is what the angels say:
Alleluia, alleluia, we will sing with them to-day.

For on the third day, as He said,
    He came again in triumph high,
And rose all glorious from the dead,
    Glittering with light and majesty.
Alleluia, alleluia, this is what the angels say :
Alleluia, Alleluia, we will sing with them to-day.

For we must die as Jesus died ;
    But now we hope with Him to rise,
And, in these bodies glorified,
    To reign with Him beyond the skies,
Alleluia, alleluia, this is what the angels say :
Alleluia, alleluia, let us sing with them to-day.

        FROM ENGLISH BOOK OF HYMNS AND CAROLS.

"Let the people praise thee, O God; let all the people praise thee."

CHRIST has arisen:
  Death is no more!
Lo! the white-robed ones
  Sit by the door.
Dawn, golden morning!
  Scatter the night!
Haste, ye disciples glad,
  First with the light.

Break forth in singing,
  O world new-born!
Chant the great Easter-tide,
  Christ's holy morn.
Chant Him, young sunbeams
  Dancing in mirth!
Chant, all ye winds of God,
  Coursing the earth!

Chant Him, ye laughing flowers,
  Fresh from the sod;
Chant Him, wild leaping streams,
  Praising your God!
Break from thy winter,
  Sad heart, and sing!
Bud with thy blossoms fair:
  Christ is thy spring.

Come where the Lord hath lain:
  Past is the gloom;
See the full eye of day
  Smile through the tomb.
Hark! angel voices
  Fall from the skies;
Christ hath arisen!
  Glad heart, arise!

E. A. WASHBURN, D.D.

"Thanks be to God
which giveth us the victory
through our Lord
Jesus Christ."

www.ingramcontent.com/pod-product-compliance
Lightning Source LLC
Chambersburg PA
CBHW031323160426
43196CB00007B/646